Life of a Tween

STORIES OF TWEENHOOD

DISHHITA JAIN

First Published in March 2023

ISBN: 978-93-5704-639-8

BLUEROSE PUBLISHERS

www.BlueRoseONE.com

info@bluerosepublishers.com

+91 8882 898 898

Cover Design:

Muskan Sachdeva

Typographic Design:

Rohit

Distributed by: BlueRose, Amazon, Flipkart

ABOUT THE AUTHOR

The author of the book "Life of Tween", is actually a tween named DISHHITA JAIN, who is just 12 years of age hailing from the city of diamonds and textile, Surat, Gujarat.

She is someone who would be called various names by all her relatives and friends like bookworm and kitaabi keeda but she never gave up her passion for reading and writing and hence this beautiful creation was written.

She would soon be going to a new place to study and raise her horizon but wishing that she never looses this gift and passion of reading and writing. This book is a gift for her from her parents(Nitin and Sweatha). All that she had practised and written during her preparations for her Entrance were compiled together into this book with the help of her teachers.

This book is a reminder that no age is too small to pursue a passion.

ACKNOWLEDGEMENTS

Writing a book is harder than I thought and more rewarding than I had ever imagined. None of this would have been possible without my first mentors, my parents who have stood by me being my first motivating factors. My mother's constant pushing and encouraging me to write has played a great role in this book turning out to be the best I could do. My parents have taught me many things which even the school could not. They are the ones with whom I have shared my secrets

I would like to thank my entire family who supported me and motivated me. I used to get irritated sometimes when my grandparents corrected me time and again but then I realised their worth when I unknowingly learnt time management and ethics from them. I cannot forget to mention to thank my younger brother Kiaan who would help me pack my bags when I would keep getting late for my classes without cribbing even once (p.s.though he keeps reminding me of this till today).

I clearly remember the day when I did not like creative writing and I had got very low marks in it, THE ones who have motivated me to write are Kanika ma'am and Megha ma'am. Kanika ma'am has kept me grounded and given me wonderful life lessons that I can never

never forget and she was the first one who believed that I could write. Thank you so much ma'am.

I cannot thank Megha ma'am enough for being the constant in editing the book, giving me ideas to write and also stay awake at midnight to proof read and edit the book. She is the one to whom the book equally belongs to. Thank you so so much Kanika ma'am and Megha ma'am. Inspite of being very busy you have treated me as your child.

I would like to thank my school DELHI PUBLIC SCHOOL, SURAT, for giving me an opportunity to enhance my creative streak and guide me at all times.

Last but not the least I would like to thank Blue rose publications who helped me publish my book because without their help I would not be able to pass my book to each one of you.

Incase I have forgotten to mention anyone else I cannot recollect I am sorry but this book is more of everyone else than mine. Thank you once again, I promise to make each one of you proud of me.

PROLOGUE

It was the breezy morning, in the month of february , when my mother and father had just come home after getting me registered for my entrance exam to be given to get in one of the top most schools in India. The moment my mom stepped inside, her eyes sparkling ing with uttermost thrill snd millions of dreams darted at me, and guess what I was expecting the lines, which I had known I had to hear till the day of my examination, "It's not going to be easy, give it everything, write every single day, Creative Writing is what are going to decide the results."

And that's when the journey commenced, every single day I used to write something, so that I could polish my writing skills, however out of those hundreds of pieces I wrote, there were these thirteen peices on which I got more than five out of ten, in rest I got less than three. What a Shame! However that's why these peices lay a special place in my heart.

When I wrote them I didn't want to preach something, I didn't want to teach something. These are just some fun experiences snd learnings, I got during my Creative Writing practice beyond's those 'Writing strategies, figures of speech, vocabulary words and writing styles'

So grab a cup of coffee or whichever beverage you like, and dive into the world of a tween!!

INTRODUCTION

" Dont do this Sara, dont eat this, dont go there ", I am sure each one of us, so called Kids can relate to these lines clearly being told to us everyday, by everyone.

We the tweens, not the KIDS nor the adults, are confused,because, we are addressed as kids most of the times but when we are told to do household chores, we are suddenly told, " you are no more a kid." So dear ADULTS,

- are we kids or
- adults or
- none of the above ?????

Here we go, once again confused !!!!!!!!!!!

I am here to share a few incidents of my life , which all we Cool (sometimes fool) tweens...... have faced sometime or the other in our life and also many life lessons learnt by me but each one of these.

CONTENTS

Chapter 1

SCARYYYYYY NIGHTTTTTTT!!!!!!

They say, "Children don't watch movies till late!", we say, "What worst will happen, will be attacked by ghosts in a nightmare!" Well, may be this story is the answer to our question.

" Oh, my God !! what a horrible creature ", thought Sara to herself. She was terrified, shivering in her boots, and with gritting teeth, she slid into a corner of her bed, hugging her brother and cursing herself, " why on this earth did I have to watch a horror movie ????"

Sara had just finished seeing a horror film and went to her room after switching off the lights to hit the hay. All of a sudden, she happened to see a shadow of a gigantic creature on her room wall.

The monster was black-colored, creepy, and terrifying. She even saw the beast sitting on her study table chair, trying to raise its hand to attack her. She screeched loudly until the entire neighborhood heard her and her parents came to her room, hearing her screams.

Her dad asked her , " Sara, what happened???? Why are you shouting ?? Uncle Sharma from the next door had also come to inquire. "

Sara told her dad that a monster was sitting near her study table on the chair in the corner of the room. Her father switched on the light and to their surprise , they all saw a pile of clothes that Sara had not cleaned up lying on her chair. They all had a hearty laugh and Sara apologized to everyone for all the hue and cry that she was responsible for .

After that day , Sara had learned:

- Never watch a horror movie before sleeping
- Always clean up the room on time
- Listen to our parents when they warn us against anything

According to them, we are KIDS and we shouldn't be watching such movies BUT we are adults and should clean up our room immediately every time.

Chapter 2

FIRST FEAR

They say, "Children learn at their own pace", but don't you believe that being a tween gives you chances to do something beyond your comfortable pace?"

Everyone has different fears like phobia for height, claustrophobia and many more. When my brain drums some memories, I realize that I also had a fear which still lingers at the back of my head even now sometimes. As I think of it now, I laugh at it but it haunted me as a kid.

The fear which I most evidently remember was the FIRST DAY OF SCHOOL. After being lectured and brainwashed by everyone at home, I was as keen as mustard to go to school, little did I know that it would turn out to be my first fear.

After getting ready in the orange and blue uniform with a pigtail oiled hair, I prayed in the temple and both my parents came to drop me to school. I was three years old and fidgety as a ball. When I think of it now I relate myself to the nervous Dobby from Harry Potter. I was so teeny holding a bag so bulky that it made me feel that

the bag had stones and not books. Never had it occurred to me that I would have to dutch down the buildings of the school, all by myself and I would have to do it all without my mom being next to me, holding my hand. I was as white as a sheet on seeing the gigantic and tall buildings of the school.

However, as they say, ' whatever happens, happens for good.' The moment I stepped inside the school premises, I was welcomed by friendly smiles of my teachers and all the helping staff. They were all very benevolent and taught us all in a friendly manner.

I made many friends in school. My mom filled my head with the right beads of values when she told me that if I go to school once, I will start loving it and have lots of fun and learning there. I came back home singing and dancing. I had many incidents and stories to tell everyone back home.

The learning that I could derive from the fear is 'WHEN YOU STEP OUT OF YOUR SHELL OF FEAR, MIRACLES HAPPEN'.

Chapter 3

TOM AND JERRYYYY. SIBLINGS

They say, "Children in tween will never realize the importance of siblings, they will know their values once they grow up!"However, is it really true? Maybe this story will change our thoughts!

Tom and Jerry is the most adorable cartoon in the world , they are watched by almost everyone and are familiar with all age groups. Same is the relation of siblings, they fight the most with one another but they are the ones who have each other's back when their mother rebukes or scolds them.

An incident of mine with my sibling which I feel extremely touched by is very close to my heart and which maybe I will never forget. This incident proves the fact that although siblings brawl a lot with each other, they are each other's first friends forever.

This incident took place on 10th August, 2022. I was preparing for my exams for a boarding school. My brother, Kiaan, was quiet and not his usual self, it was Rakshabandhan. Every year he would fight me about the

rakhi not being good and would pester me to give me a gift for Rakhi(a festival in which the sister ties a twine on the brother's hand and she gets a gift in return), but this year he was quiet and sitting in a corner of the room.

On asking many times, he finally bursted out crying, saying, " Didi, next year, if you go to a boarding school will you be able to send me a rakhi from there? I will miss you a lot." He started wailing loudly and my mother who was in the kitchen listening to him cry got emotional too. We hugged each other and after we all calmed down , our fight for the gifts and sweets started again .

This is when I realized, although initially when my brother was born , I felt a little insecure but gradually I know, we have each others back and no one else is as protective for me than MY BROTHER. I feel extremely lucky to have a sibling whom I call my Jerry and me his Tom.

Chapter 4

SMALL GESTURES AND BIGGG IMPACT !!!!!

They say , " tweens need big gifts to feel happy and good", nevertheless, this incident proves that every single small gesture of kindness changes a person drastically.

I have lately realized that small gestures do make a big difference in each one of our lives. This incident was narrated by my mother to me. I am thankful to her for teaching me and citing me such life lessons.

Her friend Suma, was a very studious girl and she always was a bookworm. One day she decided to go out to have cold coffee at a cafe with her dog, Snowy.

She took a table outside the cafe as she loved nature and wanted to enjoy the cool breeze blowing outside which could refresh her mood. The cool breeze was whistling, the birds were chirping on the lush green trees. She was totally immersed in the aura of that cafe. Far away she could also see the bustling streets filled with traffic , from which she was away and thankful. She saw a waiter, serving water at the cafe. She ordered a cold

coffee for herself. The waiter replied back with a smile . After she got her coffee , she was drinking it slowly and at her pace since she did not want to hurry and lose out on her time with the lovely nature. She had finished half her coffee when a bird perched on the tree above had dropped its droppings in her coffee. She became livid and her mood had turned bad. She started screaming at the bird but in vain . She called the waiter and spoke to him in a bad tone too. She blamed the waiter and the restaurant for allowing such creatures near their cafe but the waiter very calmly apologize even though it was not his mistake and he promised to get a fresh new cold coffee for her.

His calm demeanor soothed Suma and she was back in her good form and mood and started playing with Snowy. She thanked the waiter and even gave him a generous tip. I learnt that a small calm gesture can make the entire mood and time happy . Always be benevolent and kind to everyone, you never know what someone is going through because it costs nothing.

Chapter 5

ANIMALS: THE FACE OF MEDICAL RESEARCH

They say, "Nowadays children have found their friends in devices, however don't you believe that at any age, animals will be their friends forever?"

Animals are a part of our human race too. They deserve all the love and attention just like us Human beings. One day Sara read the news about guinea pigs, rats and many animals being used as objects of research and testing. She was aghast at this news since she loved animals .

She told her friends and other family members as she wanted to create an awareness amongst everyone. She was even more surprised to know that everyone knew about it and they all were undeterred and indifferent to this cruelty.

She thought that since the primitive age human beings have been torturing animals. Earlier they used to hunt them for their food and clothing and now they have

become so called 'civilized', so they don't hunt them for clothing but for other activities like research and testing because they can buy meat from shops and eat. She gave a speech in her school assembly on this topic that animals like monkeys, dogs, cats,rats, guinea pigs and others should not be used for this purpose instead a new way or method should be implemented or invented for the medical and cosmetic industry. She said " we should once try to be in the shoes of these animals and think of their plight and the torture they have to go through. These processes can also lead to unknown extinction of these animals which would lead to an imbalance in the natural life cycle."

All her classmates and teachers were impressed with this thought of hers and although they could not do much about it, together they decided to make a group in their school to take care of abandoned animals and be nice to them. This step at this level is the need of an hour, and with this thought I would like to end this topic by saying that each and everyone deserves love and care and attention be it animals or humans. Noone , absolutely no one deserves cruelty.

Chapter 6

BULLYING : NO MORE COOL

They say, "Making fun of each other is a part of a tween's life!" However, don't you think that it's in the age of tween, where we understand the difference between, "Friendly jokes, and bullying?"

Bullying is a very heavy word used in a light way nowadays. An incident related to it follows here.

First day of school, in the new term . I was in class five, my gang of friends was sitting together, chatting our way and talking about our vacations. We saw a new face entering our class, timid and shy. Yes, we had a new girl amidst us. She seemed to be benevolent and she decided to take the first move to be friends with 'MY GANG'. Our group was considered to be the most intelligent group of the class who would win all the competitions and all the toppers were a part of this group.

The new girl named Tina introduced herself and asked if she could come with us to the playground. All the others said a 'NO'. Then, Rina, had thought why shouldn't we make Tina do all the homework and

"

everybody else's writing work!. Poor girl Tina, being the innocent one, agreed to write the notes for everyone just to be a part of the gang. Everybody misused this innocence of Tina and gave her more work purportedly.

I was a part of the group too but somewhere deep down inside I felt guilty for treating Tina this way .One day , secretly, I had invited Tina to my abode and we decided not to tell this to anyone. We kept our friendship a secret and we decided not to listen to anyone bullying her. Tina started ignoring all the work given by the other girls. The girls got intimidated by her and started telling her that she was no longer a part of the group. Tina had now understood the ulterior motives of the girls and hence did not bother herself by this behavior. After a few days Tina and I were given a project for which we worked very hard. We realized that we needed no one to grow and bloom. Progress is a self made decision which we need to consciously take. No prizes for guessing who stood first in the project , ta!da!, It was us. The other girls realised their mistake and apologised to Tina for this act of Bullying .

I learnt that , by blowing someone else's candle we will not shine brighter.

Chapter 7

GRANDPARENTS: MY BEST FRIENDS

They say, "Children are too young to give an to their grandparents!". However, is it true? D you think there are a lot of ways we can learn as a n to showcase our love to our grandparents?"

As they say, grandparents have silver in their land gold in their heart. I love my grandparents too b my maternal or paternal.

Initially I used to get very irritated when I use to be taunted by my grandparents or my parents. had thought I had grown up and

I needed no one to tell me what to do and what not to. My dadi would keep calling me ten times to have milk when my mom would be having her tuition classes, but I would delay it by saying " just a minute". My nani would call me every night during my vacations to get my hair oiled but I used to slide away telling her that oily hair is no more cool. I feel bad when I think of how I have behaved sometimes with my elders. But one small

t made me realize that I mean the world to them
y mean the universe for me.

reezy night, I was setting my school bag for an
the next day and I realized my pen's ink had
d and I did not have an extra pen. I told my mom
t much to my surprise she scolded me and got
furious with my carelessness. I called my dad but
s in the office and by the time he would come back,
shops would shut down. I told my dadi about this,
e like a small child got equally worried for me and
up my grandfather to get a pen for me . I was
rgasted by this gesture of my grandparents. They
always given my problems equal importance as
, they are my secret keepers and my shell to hide
my parents rebuke me.

I feel lucky to be brought up in their presence and I realized that each one of us should give them time and importance. I know we are not so grown to buy them costly gifts but we can make simple memories with them like getting them acquainted with new technology, making small cards for them during their special occasions, taking them down for a stroll and many more simple things which make them feel special.

I learnt that grandparents make the home a little softer, a little kinder and a little warmer.

Chapter 8

SPORTS, MIGHT NOT BE INTERESTING FOR SOME BUT IS VERY IMPORTANT.

They say, "Nowadays for children gadgets are tiger sports", however don't you believe that it's the perfect age in which they should be inspired to take that one step towards tiger health?"

Studies are an important part of our school curriculum but sports are an important part of our life curriculum. Nowadays , children are super interested and involved in a lot of gadgets and few even have their accounts on social media which are not good for their physical and mental health. Sports help us learn many life skills as well. There is a saying to inculcate any habit or to get rid of any habit, it needs to be practiced for a minimum of 21 days after which it becomes a part of our routine and our body gets used to it.

Sometimes sports and games act as a distresser for us when we are very fatigued with continuous studying and straining our eyes. Apart from that playing sports also keep our body fit and strong. It leads to a fit body and fit

mind. Sports or physical games should be made mandatory in the daily routine of each one of us be it kids or adults. It can be imbibed into our timetable like our other activities. Sports also teach us to accept failure and be humble towards winning. It helps us to appreciate others victory and to stay undeterred by defeat.

As Virat Kohli, our famous cricket player, quoted, " sports is the only thing that taught me discipline and self control, which no amount of studies could teach." Failures teaches us much more than victory .It teaches us to work harder the next time.

It is not necessary to play any particular sport, any sport or game that interests us or daily games played in our buildings with other friends could be a good option. Being couch potatoes leads to obesity which is one of the biggest health hazards amongst children which could also be controlled by playing sports.

Chapter 9

LEARN TO TAKE HELP

They say, "Children should be taught to be independent". However, don't you believe that there's a difference between being independent and Self - dependent? Shouldn't they be just independent and not self dependent?"

It was a different day for Sara, her brother named Kiaan was being more than helpful towards her. They were the Tom and Jerry of the house but todays day started with them being the bestest of buddies. Be it starting the day with getting ready for school, holding each other's bottles, sharing his most favorite pen and many more things. Sara was very amused at this unusual behavior of Kiaan but was happy as well.

When they entered school, Kiaan was carrying Sara's bag, his own bag, their bottles, books and other necessary things of school. It was too much to carry for him but he did it relentlessly. She later got to know that his school teacher had praised his friend in front of the entire class for being helpful and caring. That day Kiaan

wanted to be that person whom the teacher adores. Sara overheard Kiaan exaggerating to his friends and teachers that he had helped doing the entire work at home, helped his mom pack the tiffin and also helped his sister in her homework. Sara called him aside and explained to him not to be so haughty but it all went in vain. He was telling his friends, " I am a hero and I can do everything that any elder can do. I can carry as many books, files and folders in one hand without dropping them down".

His friends were flabbergasted and challenged him. he accepted it!!!! He held 10 books in one hand, a basket of tiffin boxes in one hand and tried to pedal a cycle , all at the same time. Initially he felt like a hero , but after sometime he started shivering in his boots and was starting to lose his balance. His sister Sara offered to help but he refuted, his friends asked him to give up but he did not do so. As expected, he fell down and lost balance. Their tiffin box opened and the entire tiffin got spoiled and filled with dust. All the books got filthy and he too hurt himself badly. But all his friends were so helpful that they decided to share their tiffin with them so that they do not stay hungry.

Later that day, he realized that he was wrong and he apologized to all his friends. He was ashamed of his behavior. His sister told the entire story to their mom and she told them never to exaggerate and it is never too bad to ask for help when we need it.

Chapter 10

MEMORIES AND NATURE

They say, "What herculean can children do at this age to change?"Maybe this is the age where they learn the importance of small steps in order to bring change." Don't you agree?

Due to cutting down of trees, the entire ozone layer is depleting and the environment becoming highly polluted. Survival is becoming treacherous too. Soon in some decades, if this continues, we would have to find another planet to live on. This is something we all know, however somewhere it is quite known to us, that those old trees and the games we play around and under them have given lots of beautiful memories that we can cherish for our lifetime. One such incident happened with Sara too.

" Oh! My God, they are going to cut my most favourite tree and the best part of my house" said Sara in distress. It was their banyan tree next to their house which the local municipal corporation was planning to cut down because it was blocking the road. Sara and her family

had many memories attached to it. She used to go sit under it when she had a fight with her sibling, they used to swing together there, they had family picnics under its shade, they also climbed on its branches to hide from their homeworks.

Sara coaxed her parents to talk to the local authorities to let the tree stay there. She even wrote a letter to the corporation and got the signatures of all her other friends and their parents to not cut down the tree. They played sadly that day under the tree thinking that it is no more going to be there after a few days.

Later in the evening, Sara's dad had announced to the kids that their petition had been accepted. They all jumped in jubilation and danced in joy on hearing this. They thanked the municipal commissioner and the local officers profusely. They also thanked their parents for being so supportive in this mission of theirs.

We learn that be it very small, every memory needs to be treasured and every possibility should be tried to save it.

Chapter 11

MISJUDGEMENT AND THEN REPENTANCE

They say, "Children are too young to decide what's right and what's wrong." However, don't you agree that it's quite easy for them to learn this, provided we teach them the right way."

Excitement was in the air when it was our D-day to go for a vacation. We were going for a family trip to Darjeeling. We had packed lots of eatables since it was a train trip and we had to pack woolen clothes since it was freezing there. We were the most excited out of the lot. Dad also carried a camera to click many photos and he was very fond of it.

We reached the station just on time inspite of being told many times by our dad that we should reach half an hour early. Luckily we found a porter to help us with the luggage. Our train was already on the platform and we ran to our coach number A1. It was night journey so the coach was dark and so my mom switched on her mobile light to guide us to our seats. Our train was just about to start and then my dad noticed that the porter had not

yet boarded our luggage. There was panic and we all rushed down to the platform to search for the porter, but he was no where in sight. He searched and searched for the porter but we couldnt find him. We all got down since we could not travel without our luggage. My parents had gone to the station patrol service department to lodge a complaint against the porter. They were making a complain and we were waiting outside the enquiry room for our parents.

All of a sudden we spotted the porter who had taken our luggage and ran towards him thinking that we were heroes and caught him red handed. We called our parents and all four of us ran towards the porter and confronted him. We scolded him and called him a thief and we also scared him telling that we have complained against him. He got very scared and petrified on hearing this. He softly told us that he had already put the luggage under the seat number mentioned by us in our coach. We went him to check and yes the luggage was all set properly and neatly right under the our seats. We realised that we had got into the wrong coach number, instead of A2 we got into A1 and mistook someone else's seats to be ours. We apologised to the porter and realised that we should never judge someone wrongly until we know the truth. We had an adventurous start to our journey and had a hearty laugh thinking about this incident. We had a joyful time in Darjeeling and we clicked many photographs to keep as memories but this

incident is a memory which we will all never forget and it would need no photographs to remember.

Chapter 12

ANGER MANAGEMENT:

They say, "Children don't understand how to be patient, they are like transparent bottles, they will flow out whatever is in their heart, they are kids after all!". However, don't you agree that by not learning at the right time, children can have an equal amount of difficulty in handling their anger with maturity, when they turn adults?

Everybody gets angry and different people have different coping mechanisms to curb their anger. In ancient times many kings and queens used to have an anger room called 'KOP BHAWAN', when they used to get angry or furious they would detach themselves from that situation and go to that room to cool themselves down by doing the things which soothed them. But nowadays people break things, say abusive words and try to bring down others which spoils the relationship with the other person.

Disagreements and arguments are healthy if taken place in a good spirit and in a structured manner. Healthy

criticism leads to improvement and growth in an individual. Sometimes people bottle up their anger and do not discuss it with anyone which leads to the emotion coming out in a wrong and destructive way.

When Sara, gets angry, she goes to her room balcony with her favourite headphones, ipad and her best friend(her book). When she gets livid and disconcerted, she likes to move away from that place and take time to think about the whole situation and then get back. Her balcony is very capacious and she feels at peace amidst the wind blowing and the sounds of the chirping birds. She can also see her building playground, lush green trees and many children playing on the slides which make her rethink her reaction to the situation.

She teaches us a very important lesson that anger is a weakness and we should try and control it as we tend to do or say many unwanted things which we may regret later. So whenever one gets angry take a time out, rethink and then react.

Chapter 13

THINK RETHINK REACT

They say "Children must always be careful, and must run their brains, against something which their parents have taught them." However, don't you think, that children should be taught to take right steps according to what their heart says, apart from just being careful?

It was that happy time of the day when Sara was getting back from school. She was so tired but her excitement took over since she had so many tales and stories to tell her mom about the day in school. When she was strolling on the footpath, sunk in her thoughts somebody tapped on her shoulder. Initially , she was aghast and flabbergasted to see an old man in tattered clothes who was asking for her help. She got so scared that she thought of running away from there. She had already been warned by her parents about the different mishaps that could happen so she needed to be very careful. The old man looked very miserable and he seemed as if he had not eaten or bathed for years. He started to wail loudly and was asking for food. He told Sara that he came to her city from a village. His son had bought him here and

left him on the station and never came back. He had also told that his mobile has been stolen and did not have his son's address.

Sara was a smart cookie but in this situation she did not know what to do. Helping him would be a big big big risk which she did not want to take, but somewhere down the heart she was a benevolent and a well brought up child so she felt bad for the old man .She saw a police officer on the other side of the street and decided to take help from him. The police officer did his duty and he made a few calls to the necessary people. Meanwhile Sara had also called up home to let her parents know she was safe was reaching home in few minutes.

Within half an hour the old man was taken to the police station and the description of his son and family was also noted. He was dropped to his son's abode and he was very grateful to Sara and the police officers who did a great job .

After reaching home Sara narrated the entire incident to her parents. They got scared but then they also felt proud of Sara when she received a bravery award from her city for the gesture she had done. We should be careful while addressing strangers but never loose humanity.

Chapter 14

SURPRISE TIME !!!!!

They say, "Children need materialistic gifts to be happy, and there is nothing wrong if they forget their mother's and father's birthday, they are kids after all!" However, don't you agree that kids are more hungry for love and attention, and they can also be taught to give that love and special attention?

Sara got up with a broad smile that day , it was a very special day for her. She did not have to check her calendar because she had been counting days for today, since it was her BIRTHDAY. She had school that day so she brushed her teeth and got ready for school. As soon as she stepped out of her room she could hear all her family members wishing her a very happy birthday. She took the blessings from her grandparents, parents and a tight hug from her brother. They all gave her many gifts and she was the attention taker that day. Breakfast, lunch and dinner were all decided by her a day in prior. She had her breakfast and kept a few chocolates for her comrades.

She went to school exhilarated and was on cloud nine. All her friends and teachers wished her and she had a lovely day at school. As the school bell rang, she expected all her friends to stay back for some time with her and talk to her about her plans for the day but she noticed that everyone was in a haste to leave for their abodes. She had no choice but to leave early as well.

When she reached home, she was aghast on seeing the door of her house ajar and nobody was in sight. She called out for her mom, but she was nowhere to be seen. The entire house was unusually dark and not a noise coming from anywhere. She got petrified and all sorts of negative thoughts had popped up in her head. She called up her dad but he did not answer his phone. She ran down to her neighbours' house but none of them opened their door as well. She sat down thinking what must be done. She sadly went inside her room to change and think of what needs to be done and then suddenly all the lights turned on and all her friends and family started to sing a loud birthday song for her. She got teary eyed as she least expected the surprise that everyone had planned for her.

Now she realized why all her friends were in a haste, why her dad did not answer his phone and why none of her neighbours' opened their door. She thanked everyone profusely and was feeling truly blessed to have so many people love her and wanting her day to be extra special.

Finally she realized that it only takes one moment of care and love to make anyone feel special and loved and we should never miss an opportunity to make anyone feel special because none of the gifts stay with us forever but the memories that are created together are ones that stay in our heads and hearts for a lifetime.

Chapter 15

NOONE BETTER THAN BEST FRIENDS

They say, "Children have their favorites, and they will always listen and respect the ones who hold a special place in their hearts." And yes, they are absolutely right!!

My Nani and Nanu are my best friends:

As Sara mentioned earlier, grandparents are someone who have silver in their hair but gold in their hearts. Sara'sNani (maternal grandmother) is very close to her from the time she was born. Whenever her mom would take her to their house, Sara would always sleep with her nanima. She was the one with whom Sara would share all her thoughts and stories.

Sara would resent applying oil in her hair but whenever she used to go there for their vacations, her nani would always convince her and apply oil every single day. She was the only one who could convince Sara into doing anything. Whenever Sara would go there she would make all sorts of special delicacies that Sara and her brother liked. That was the only place where Sara and

her brother would never get scolded and had the liberty to watch television for the entire day.

I adored applying nail polish on her nails as she was a diva and loved pampering herself. Sara got this gait of self care from her nani. Her nani loved pampering herself just like Sara. After lunch they would all sit down on the cool floor where Sara would lay down near her nani ma and her nanu would make plans for the evening. Her maternal grandparents' town had a lovely beach nearby so they would go there everyday and sit by the sand and enjoy the lovely corn and bhel there.

Their nanu would list down the new places that they should go every evening and the midnight pizzas that he would order for them without their mom complaining was a privilege they longed for and waited for every vacation. Summer vacations were the most awaited times for Sara and her brother.

They shared a great rapport with both their grandparents (maternal and paternal) who loved them and pampered them. They even rebuked them if they went wrong but most of times they only got lots and lots of love from all four of them.

This chapter is solely dedicated to DADA, DADI and NANI, NANI. I love you all and I promise to make you all proud of me one day.

EPILOGUE

"Dishita, it's already 12! Tomorrow's a big day, just turn in, chop chop!!" bellowed my mother on one of these chilly nights November month, 2022. When the entire city is drowning in the fervour of Diwali, and all the mothers are involved into deep home cleaning. My mother is shuddering with stress, and has been sleep deprived for more than three months.

Well I am happy that after tomorrow she will sleep like a monk after ages. Wondering what's tomorrow, it's the day when I am heading to Dheradun for my entrance exam. Well, if I give you a reality check, then let me confess, even my tummy is giving me jitters, and even my nerves are giving me shivers. But hey, why am I writing all of this, the train is tomorrow, I deserve a peaceful sleep today!

Well, the chapter which you will read last is one of the last peices of my practice, so if you find any error while reading them, please forgive me. I am honestly feeling anxious by even pondering the experience I will have after two days. I don't care if I loose or win, I just care that I don't stumble while speaking, don't fiddle while writing and don't twiddle while reading!!

And the clock has already struck 12:15 AM, it's time for me to turn in. Buy the way, by the time I come back, you

all must have already grabbed the copies, I hope that I live upto to your expectations by being a Welhamite ofcourse, but even in respect of my writing. Please wish me luck, and I shall see you all soon!!!

Good night! and Happy reading!